Pieces of me

Rachel Aquino

for
Who once was my first love

The single most important thing

"This one time I painted a living room with a girl. This was a handful of years back. It was about eight months before the huge, flame-out of a breakup. That day, though? That day we painted the living room? It was pretty uneventful. We painted my parents living room for $50 between us and a pizza. That was it. I think we watched Anchorman or something after that.

But it still holds as on of the most indelible memories I have. Don't get me wrong, I'm not still in love, it happened, it was good, it ended, and we've both moved on. But I'll never forget that day. Because it's never, in the long run, about the grand gestures. You can fly across the world and show up on her doorstep with a rose in your teeth and a ring in a little velvet box but I can guarantee you that - more often than not - she's going to remember the time you built the birdhouse in the back yard, or what have you, a whole lot more.

Life wasn't meant to be taken in large movements. The next day will inevitably arrive, you'll sleep, and the moment will have passed. But when you have a hundred thousand small moments, you can step back and appreciate the picture a lot more than metaphorically blowing your load on some grand moment that, in all honesty, look, you're not Bruce Fucking

Springsteen, you're not going to be able to blow everyone's mind every single night. You're not Romeo and/or Juliet. There's no reason to drink the poison together in some flame-out gesture. So that leaves us with the small stuff. It's all about the detail.

That's what love is. Attention to detail.

And the moment will end. And then things will get boring. And it might get a little quiet. And it might all end horribly. And you might hate each other at the end. And you might walk away from each other one day and never speak again. But that's just how it goes.
But she'll remember the time you held the door open for her on your first date.

She'll remember the time you laughed at her impression of the landlady.
She'll remember the time you stayed up all night that first time.
She'll remember the small things a lot longer than the big ones.

But everything ends. And I'll tell you why you have to make the small things, the small moments count so much more:
One day, probably a while longer from now, when old age takes ahold of someone, she might just only remember your smile.
Everything you ever did together, every second,

every moment, every beat, every morning spent in bed, every evening spent together on the sofa, all of that - gone. *Everything you ever did will be **reduced to the head of a pin**.* She won't remember your name. She'll just remember your smile, and she'll smile. She won't know why. It's a base, gut reaction. But she'll smile, uncontrollably, and it will come from somewhere so deep as to know that you touched her on a primal, honest, and true level that no scientist, scholar, or savant could ever *begin* to explain. There is no more. There is nothing else. There is just this: She'll remember your smile, and she'll smile.
And you know what? That's all that really matters in the end."

- Anonymous

I hold this story so deeply within my heart, for it reminded me of what makes love so significant. We tend to take so many little things for granted in search for "*more*" that we don't take the time to appreciate the little things that create such a powerful and delicate love. I remember all the *grand* gestures he did, all the picture perfect moments that swept me from under my feet, and they all mean so much but In the end I craved the most innocent parts of our relationship.
The little details that were engraved into my mind through memories..
It made letting go so exquisitely painful

I yearned the small intimate *things*
The way you use to look at me
The way you caressed my hand
The way you drew circles on my back so slowly,
so softly
The way we were unquestionably in love
The small innocent parts of you will never
escape me
Your silly and dorky quirks
The way you scrunch up your nose when you're
trying to be 'Mr.cool guy'
When you tried to crush that cheese-it on the
floor but completely missed
When you surprised me with an easter present
and exclaimed "happy valentines day!"
The typos in all the love letters you wrote me
The way you'd spell "squedule" instead of
"schedule"
So imperfectly perfect

If I could go back and change anything, I
wouldn't of overlooked these small things, I'd
appreciate every last detail of your being, love
you properly from the beginning, with no pride.

Only if I *really knew* that
Love is attention to the detail
-
These poems are pieces of me
Hopefully you will find a piece of you

Love

Passion

Loss

Pain

Acceptance

Healing

You

Why does the sun set through
the glaze of our eyes
Time gliding by
dancing with the effulgent moon
and secretly adoring the
substantial shine of the stars
-

Why does the earth spin, or weather change
Here we are looking up in grief
as the soul of the
galaxies looks down with great compassion
We hid behind our burdens in fear
waiting for something to give us aspiration
Waiting until the end of time for a
genuinely tender and benevolent soul
to bring harmony to the vulnerable
and delicate fire within us; spirit
Life is an aesthetically exquisite hell, ironically
divine.
-

When I look up into the heavens
I see your name engraved into the cerulean
skies
with the mendacious stars

Beauty

He was beautiful in every way
From the way his eyes were synchronized
with the luminous glow of the galaxies
to the tender touch of his hand
His embrace
How could the simplicity of an atom
build such perfection,
molded from the core of the heavens..
You are a once in a lifetime infatuation
that the stars whisper among each other
Never to be heard of again
To be lost with the sand brushed by the
elegant flow of the unceasing river
I know males aren't suppose to be beautiful...
but he was beauty and beauty itself

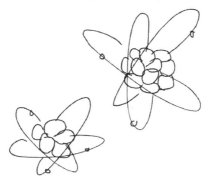

Balance

I believe friendship is unbreakable.
Love is powerful and strong,
but is fragile and breaks easily
It leaves heavy scars without friendship.
What's important is the core of love, happiness,
and the little things that hold it together.
The long walks, the insignificant arguments
about who ate the last piece of chocolate,
Little chats about culture, art, music, and
literature.
True friendship is what holds it all together,
and all that matters in the end.
Honestly without it... Love is nothing.
Nothing but a word, we give meaning to it.
Our bond, our friendship.
There is a subtle difference with being in love
and loving someone.
Affection does matter,
but must and should be equally balanced.

Promises

"I make this solemn promise to you:
To be your lover when you need to be loved,
Your doctor when you are ill,
Your army when you go to war,
Your umbrella when life rains down on you,
Your rock when you get weary,
Your shield when you need defense,
Your spirit when you are drained,
Your pillow when you need to rest,
Your voice when no one can hear you,
Your ear when no one will listen,
Your comfort when you feel pain,
Your hero when you are under duress,
Your sunshine when darkness falls,
Your answer when questions arise,
Your inspiration to overcome obstacles,
Your hand to hold when you are frightened,
Your kiss that wakes you everyday,
and your "I love you" each and every night.
I am yours... all of me."

It's just life
People betray you,
Sometimes you work hard for nothing in return,
You fail at something you've worked hard for,
Life within itself will break you.

-words from a dear friend

The little things

You're a masterpiece.
I'll never get tired of looking at you.
You're so effortlessly beautiful in every way,
and there's nothing I can do.
Your free flowing curls
that seem to glide with every step you take.
The creases your face forms when you smile,
The way your lips fold,
Your piercing emerald eyes, which carry pieces
of me
Every last detail of your being is engrained into
my soul,
Fermented in my bones.
Your soul is iridescent
You are so beautiful, yet so oblivious of it
And that is why I know
that I will helplessly be in love
with every part of you for the rest of my life

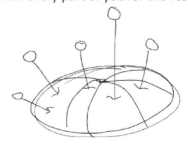

"I wish I wasn't so quiet when we talked, and I wish I knew all the right things to say. But if I were to hook up a projector into my brain and rolled it like a movie then I guess this is what you would see. A whole bunched up tape of memories filled away, unorganized, and plentiful.

Love scattered on the floor filling all the empty spaces In between, all the cracks all the air pockets. Your name not written on the walls but the floor and ceiling. I so wish to be the best in everything I do including you. I hope that you can see through my quiet nature and somewhat awkward appearance and when you look in my eyes I hope you see the colors racing around because my mind is injected with feelings of love every time you are close to me. It makes me feel like I'm floating and watching myself in third person asking, "is this even real?" Because how could a guy like me... End up with a girl like you? Someone as beautiful and talented, stunning and ambitious. I'm just a runner in life pushing through and somehow I ended up pushing my way into the most beautiful thing on this planet, you.

I can say it over and over again but the word "thankful" just doesn't hold up to what I actually feel with you. I want it to be a thousand letters long and have a meaning deeper than the ocean because Rachel I am so thankful to have you in my life. I wish to be a part of your beautiful story for as long as I can, so that one day we will be able to combine our books and write side by side, creating one book devoted to us"

-here's our book love

Your puzzle

"I had spent so many years leering into the vast
darkness of night.
I was searching for the answer that complete
the puzzle of my life.
Like so many nights before, waiting for a
shooting star to wish upon.
And every time i found one i wished for
someone like u too come along.

I used to lie in bed at night and dream of you.
And would fall asleep feeling so alone and
awaking as i always do.
To my empty bed with pillows piled to hug like
you were near.
And i would feel so sad inside knowing, it was a
dream you were not here.

So back to heavens skies I would go at night,
and stare up at the stars.
And feeling so small almost at all, wishing on my
shooting star from afar but after my long cold
nights of searching through the skies.

On a cold September I received the most amazing surprise.

The surprise was meeting you my love, my angel from above.
You shower me with tenderness and uncontested love.
You give to me the strength I need to be a better man.
And to know what love really is, you help me understand.

Your smile sets my soul ablaze, and your voice carries like a song.
You lift me up from feeling when everything goes wrong.
You complete my puzzle and were the piece I could not find.
But now together in life I cannot get you off my mind.
You are in my dreams at night and my thoughts throughout the day.
I never thought I could love somebody in every single way.
I was destined to meet you and that is true too see"

Our bond

"I feel as though one of the purposes of my life is to care and love you. We grew together, causing us to get closer and closer until one day we finally met at one point. And that to me is how real love stories start, they start with a bond, and the bond grows.

Yes the ups and downs can be hard, but there's something more, something that we can only feel, that really makes us individual from everyone else. And that bond that we have is something so precious, and so magnificent, that realizing we have it brings tears to my eyes. Rachel you have not only showed me happiness, you showed me who I am. You showed me that I'm more than just a average boy and you show me what true love really means.
Some days I just lay in my bed and think about all the lessons and great moments I have learned with you. It feels like a life time, and that statement being said I can just imagine how much more we will grow together and flourish together throughout our lives."

Beautiful moments

We lay on the rooftop of your house
engulfed by the hazel sunset
Your soft breaths down my neck
Your arms tenderly embracing me
Our hands intertwined
Our souls swaying with the breeze
I could *feel*
I *felt* you
Your beauty was timeless
We were infinite, we could be forever
In that moment I realized
I was so madly deeply and helplessly in love

Your kisses

Kisses which sparked cosmic energy into my
heart
Seeming to make it beat again
You made me *alive*
Your lips, interlocked with mine
A perfect fit
My lips were made for your lips
-
I was made for you
But you were not made for me

Wallflower

He was a wallflower
watching from the sidelines
Not a word escapes his lips
but there's a luminous fire inside of him
His passion burns
Silent screams
An olden touch
He was an echo from a other star

Bitter honey

You never know it's your last moment until it's
all over
I feel our last moment in such clarity
So potent I could taste the honey that seeps
through the holes of my memory
So sweet it hurts
"Don't forget about me.." I pleaded
"I won't" you promised
Your lips met mine for the last time
I held you, and embraced your lovely body for
the last time
I watched you walk away
Little did I know, you wouldn't come back

The ghost of you

I walk the halls past oceans
of meaningless people
All I can see is the ghost of who you once were
Visions of what we once were
I turn to my right
I see *us*
You look down at me with your perplexing eyes
holding my hands in yours
Your gentle grasp *touching* my soul
I turn to my left
My vision now glossed by the memory of you
I see *us*
I'm looking up at you with my longing eyes
Craving your touch
Make me feel alive again

Where did it all go?

Quiet sailor

He ventures the sea
Travels oceans
Travels souls
A passionate heart that radiates
to everyone he touches
Ironically introverted
Never stopping for anyone
He must *go*

The fault in our stars

The sun lays to rest
The moon meets the sky
Stars illuminate the world we share
I lay in bed, eyes heavy, heart content
as you read to me
I am all consumed in your soft voice
Your voice caressing my mind to sleep
-

"my love, I cannot tell you how thankful I am
for our little infinity. I wouldn't trade it for the
world.
You gave me a forever within the numbered
days,
and I'm gratefu—"

Round top

I wish I took the time to love you more closely
Forgive you more closely
Embrace you more closely
Look at you more closely
-
I woke up slowly
to the feeling of your soft lips on my face
My body slowly awaked as
you lifted me off the bed
My face buried in the nape of your neck
Your scent flooding our proximity
Your sweet scent, so aesthetically unforgettable
I saw your gleaming face as I opened my eyes
In that moment I fell in love all over again

And I'm sorry

Ignited

You kindle emotions in me that I don't have
names for yet

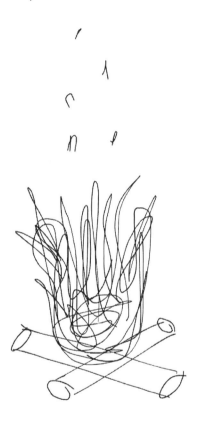

Loving you

It was a storm in the ocean
with the most extravagant highs
that have never been felt before
to the most devastating lows that almost feel
like I'm drowning
-
A part of me thinks it's worth it
I want to be in this storm
because the abundant happiness you gave is
something that cannot be given by anyone else
Including myself
-
But another part of me sighs in relief that
the storm is finally over and is content with
the lovely rainbow it has left

Did you forget?

The tiny blue cottage we were suppose to share
Long beach shores that we have yet to walk
Growing old, continuing to be in unconditional
love
Our now non-existent late night embraces
-
The future you forgot

I wonder

Sometimes I wonder, what if we met 5 years
from now?
Would I fall in love all over again?
Would the walls I meticulously built brick by
brick come crashing down?
Would you recall the small intricate details of
what make me?
Because I know I'll never forget you
-
Maybe we will be completely different people
with no trace of each other's touch to our once
pure souls
Like a planet once thrived with life, love, and
energy
Now extinct of everything there once was,
leaving no affirmation that anything was ever
there in the first place
Shouts dwindled into quiet whispers
Magnificent songs slipped into slow hums
-
Sometimes I wish that fate will bring us
together one day again. Maybe we will be ready
for each other

Sushi choo-choo

I watch the assembly line of hundreds types of
sushi rolling past me
Waiting patiently for my favorite to cross
I spot it from the conner of my eye
Out of everything, your favorite spicy tuna roll
sits next to mine
There it was.. the infamous spicy tuna roll and
Philadelphia roll that
we've eaten on so many dates
Sitting side by side
In content, I think, what a coincidence
The small things in everything I do
always seem to remind me of you

November 23, 2015

When I look into your eyes all the lies,
seemingly deceitful manners
and fraudulent dispositions suddenly vanish
Leaving a constellations of exquisite intimacy
and divine passion,
The emerald and gold jewels intertwining with
the effervescent galaxy
lures the ceaseless and unfathomable
tenderness I have for you,
Complex
Intense
Cavernous
Enigmatic
Indecipherable

The pain

Thinking about you hurt. Watching at you hurt. How did this all happen? Is all love temporary? Promises shattered, expectations always let down. Not everything was bad. You were the biggest high and low in my entire life. I'll never fully and truly understand what happened and why you don't love me anymore. I just accept that it's just life. Nothing is ever permanent. I was a fool to of thought you would never leave me, to think we were forever.

Your new relationship will never be close to par as what we once were. You just can't *love* her how you once *loved* me. I'm scared, and I'm still lost. I don't know if I'll ever really love again. Im a slave to the seeds of "love" you planted in my soul. I want to be free, and break these chains you have locked on me. Every time I feel free, the feelings I thought I had forgotten ricochet back. It's exhausting. You use to be my *soul mate*, but soon you'll be a stranger. I know I could've done better, and been better for you, but you threw me away anyways... I guess I wasn't worth it to you. When you left you took a piece of me. The saddest part of this love is you'll never really appreciate the things I did for you, or value my love. It's hard to accept how people change. Your heart changed, and you've changed me. I never thought you would.

"April 21, 2014
I fell in love with all of you

I didn't just fall in love
With the best of you like
The way your eyes light up the room
The way your laugh makes me smile
The way your hand fits in mine
The way your personality stands out
The way your smile gives me butterflies
Or the way your body moves

I fell in Love with all of you

I fell in love with your scars
The way you make sarcastic remarks
The way you feel helpless at 2am
The way you cry about the past
The way you can sometimes get angry
Or the way you get bugs in your mind

I fell in love with all of you

I fell in Love with the great in you

And i fell in love with the "bad" you see in
yourself
But the bad you see is the great i see
Because i love every part of you
Every bit

I fell in love with all of you

Rachel Lazatin Aquino

I promise you my deepest love, my fullest
devotion, my tenderest care through the
pressures of the present and the uncertainties
of the future. I promise to be faithful to you. I
promise to love you, to commit to you and
support you.I promise to respect your unique
talents and abilities, to lend you strength for all
of your dreams. You have shown me what love
feels like and for that I thank you. You are
everything I need and at this moment I know all
of my dreams have come true. I thank god for
you, for all your love and constant tenderness. I
know that our love is precious and I promise to
be here forever and always. My heart will be
your shelter and my arms will be your home. As
I have given you my hands to hold, I give you
my life to keep" -J

Here I am august 28 2016, and this is why I question *"love"*.

Delete

Forget all the faces that you miss
Forget all the pain that resides in your heart
Forget the feelings
Stop wondering
Stop blaming
Start living

Close

I knew when I met you
You were the closest I'd ever get
to being close to anyone

Pathetic

You were so pathetically charming
Soul so pure
Laughter so innocent
That's why I was so pathetically in love with you

I knew, and I know this feeling
will *linger*
until I'm old and content
Inhabiting my heart for the rest of my life
Dormant but *alive*
Ceasing to subside
Waiting for you to come back

-When you said we were "still so young"

Safe house

Your arms were home
Being in them all the anxiety, insecurities
and overwhelming adversities
vanished away
Washed away like white sand
on the shore of the lavish sea
You were the only person in this world
who could put my monsters to rest
You were my safe house in this world
full of hurt and chaos
Now you are my chaos

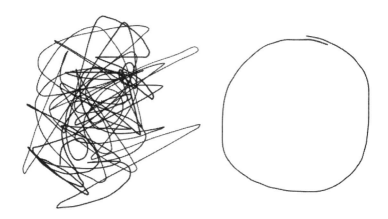

Someone who will love me unconditionally
and unquestionably
Someone who puts their pride aside
to forgive me
Make me feel loved
Make me feel *fulfilled*
A tender soul
Reliable
Understanding
Compassionate
Forgiving
Wise
Who will hold me up when I can't for myself
Who will hold my hand when I'm scared
Who will undoubtedly be there
Ready to catch me when I fall

-who I need to love me

I wish you never stopped
wanting me

-that's just how the cards play out

Your own hero

You must love yourself
before you can expect anybody else to
You must cherish yourself
Need yourself
Sometimes you'll have to be your own hero
You'll have to save yourself
Because honey,
he just doesn't give a damn
-
Pick up the scattered piece of your heart
Gently place them back together
Make the pieces fit together yourself,
For yourself
Not because you want to,
but because it's necessary

You

You consume me
Again, all I can think about is you
I find myself looking through old photos
and passing by ones of you
from your birthday September 30, 2015
Looking at *you*
Not the person you appear to be
Not your surface self
I was looking at *you*
The you that nobody else has seen
The one that wore my silly Minnie Mouse ears
just to make me giggle
The one who is soft on the inside
and tears up at my heart felt letters
I find myself looking at *you*
and I think to myself
"God help me.. I love him so much."
I love you so much it brings me to tears

-12/3/15 9:25 AM

Rollercoaster

I can feel myself slipping
from my own finger tips
And there is nothing I can do about it
I've slowly lost all control
Why am I confined by you
Get out of my head
Stop consuming me
Loving you is a never-ending roller coaster
Except I'm the only one riding..
This love only makes me dizzy

Desensitizing love

Afraid to feel too deeply
Afraid to say too much
Afraid to show people the abundance
in which I care
Exposing my vulnerability
-
Don't let the world harden your spirit
Don't let beautiful moments slip away
from the fear and scars of rejection
Take pride in the intense love you have to give
Not many people can love like you

Nothing yet everything makes sense with you
Loving you was blissfully agonizing
You are a rose
Breathtaking at sight
but painful to touch
All I can do now is adore you from a distance
Secretly
Quietly
It's a lovely kind of pain

-paradoxical love

Bandaging the scars you left
A temporary fix
Filling the emptiness you've created in me
As I look at the stranger beside me
I realized some things are easier
to give away than my heart

-Temporary company

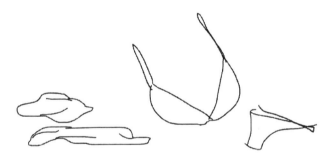

Untouched

Sometimes I think it would be better to not feel
What would my life be like if you hadn't
touched my soul?
If the world never *touched* me
Still so innocent
Still full of falsified hope
Craving the sweet aroma of love
Ignorant of the reality the world batters
into your soul
Would I be free?

I didn't fall
I walked into love with you
Meticulously
Slowly
Knowingly
and all at once
Oh, I was so scared of falling

-Soon I realized I didn't have a choice

Your lips

Your lips had me in awe
Like tasting honey for the first time
So dangerously sweet
I could never get tired of them
Feeling them
Tasting them
I found my new addiction

Changed

Will I ever be able to love anybody
like I loved you?
In search for something
to make me feel alive again
Surrounded by bodies
ceasing *intimacy*
Will I forever be closed up?
With colossal walls built so thoroughly
from the pain you've left
Fearful to become vulnerable
like I was for you
Will I forever be changed?

Intimacy

Connecting with a soul
A bond which fuses each other
together in this abundant world
The ability to *touch* someone
without touching them
The purest forms being so rare
So breathtakingly beautiful
Humans crave it
Aching for it
Honey dripping from their lips

I was tired of feeling less than whole
when I was with you
I would've rather been alone
than to hold onto our
distant touch
faded passion
Our diminishing lukewarm love

-my final goodbye

empty

12/17/16

Discomforting stares
Unspoken tension
You held her like you use to hold me
Benevolently with your tender touch
Looked at her with the same
perplexing eyes you looked at me with
Caressed her skin the way I engrained
into your being
Can she taste the perpetual traces of me on
your lips?
-

It was same demonstrative play
but with a different actress
I watch as my role had been replaced
Every line, every part, every movement
But I felt *nothing*

I wish I could crack your beautiful skull open
Break into your mind
See the treacherously exquisite things
hidden in the constellation of your
thoughts
-

My eyes often meet your alluring eyes
and I can't help but wonder
What thoughts
What emotions
my eyes provoke inside of you

-curiosity

Enough

I could never get *enough* of you
My soul had a restless desire for you
Every second I spent with you felt timeless
Could I *feel* you just a little longer
Could I kiss you just a little longer
Could I hold you just a little longer
But a little longer still wasn't *enough*

Pain has deep roots
Like an unwanted weed
It will always come back
unless removed by
the roots
The origin of your suffering
-

You must dig deep
Forgive them
Forgive yourself
To set yourself free

-part of the healing process

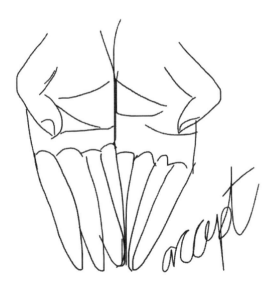

I wish you'd take me on a date again
That you'd ask to spend more time with me
That you'd show me your affection
That you'd listen to my feelings and understand
That you wouldn't have so much pride
That you were more interested in me
That you'd act proud to have me

-things I wish, but won't say out loud

12/21/15

He use to have a thousand beautiful dimensions
But now faded into a two dimensional reality
I like to believe the old him I knew is still there
And sometimes I see *him*
I treasure those moments
I love him for every part
but I deeply long for *him*
-
You told me to be strong for you
but I'll be strong for myself
-
The way you hold me is like home
You make me feel so safe
yet completely vulnerable
You brought my pieces back together
but also broke them apart
So bitter sweet
-
I wish you the absolute best my friend

Maybe

Maybe one day you'll realize
One day you'll see
all that we could've been
In two years
In twenty years
Maybe you'll look back
and think exactly what I am
-
You'll wonder why you
gave up on someone
who would've have given you
anything and everything
Maybe you'll realize
you could've had everything
but chose nothing

Genuine love finds you
Never chase
Never beg
Just live

-the journey

Life is about trusting your feelings
Finding happiness
Taking chances
Putting your heart on the line
Risking it all
Learning from past experiences
and realizing how
the days and people change

-what we live for

Naked

I fear people seeing my vulnerability
Peeking into my soul
My heart
Read my most intimate thoughts
that have been hidden so deeply inside of me
Hidden from the world
but now *exposed*

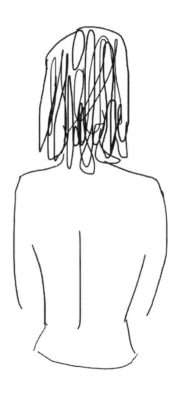

"you should be very a confident girl because
your outward and inward appearance
is always very beautiful"

-is this real or just what I wanted to hear?

Mellow and lethargic soul
My heart seemed to beat
a little slower than everybody else
Drowning in this sea of emptiness
while I watch everybody else take
their sufficient breaths
-

Shuffling through a dark tunnel
with no radiance in sight
Frozen in time
with no movement
How do I escape?
Chained by the thoughts and insecurities
I call monsters from within me
Self blame, self conscious, alone
There is no hope
Is there?

-unknowingly depressed

Acceptance

My soul has been awakened
I can finally see
Through the stages of grief
I've broken the chains which
have confined my soul for too long
-
I've regained the lost pieces of me
I've found myself
I've learned that acceptance is the key
Acceptance is what truly sets you free
I am ready to *live*

After everything

"I just read your card, and I am absolutely speechless. I've never read anything so beautiful and just the exact words to bring me to tears and have the most amount of joy that I can have. I can't explain to you how important and how honored I feel to be such a friend to you that you would give me something like this, so simple in it's entirety, but I can't explain to you how it just filled my heart to the brim with unexplainable emotions. You are truly a gift from God in my life, you are the biggest beacon in my life that guides me through the thickest fog. There are absolutely no words in this world to thank you enough for being in my life. I'm so so blessed, so truly blessed to have you by my side through thick and thin. And that is all I could ever ask for and that is all I hope to do for you. You do not understand the emotions you give me, they are unlike anything I've ever felt and i feel like you have the hands of God and are able to reach inside me and flip my heart on. I'm so grateful, so very grateful to have a best friend like you

I'm so baffled by your existence

How can there be a person so perfect in every way like you?
You are so pure and so bright I am just so overly blessed to be a part of your life and you be a part of mine"

-November 28, 2015 10:15 PM

Lost

Molding myself to compliment
your shape
I forgot my true form
I lost myself trying to chase you
-
Focusing so much on your needs
I never stopped to tend to my own
Sufficient to your love
I forgot how to
truly love myself
-
You were my identity
and I was now nothing
but a misfit toy
-
I ask myself after you left
"who am I?"
In that moment, I realized how lost
I truly was
-
Who am I without him?

Innocent memories

I wrapped my pointer finger around
your gracefully flowing golden-brown curls
Twirling lock by lock
Pressing them against my thumb
-

Observing every intricate
movement you made
I don't think I've *seen*
anything as vividly as I *saw* you
in this innocent moment of love
-

It's easy to be mesmerized
by beautiful things
But you were more than beautiful
You personified the meaning of beautiful
You *embodied* beautiful
-

I caressed your skin
Sending soft shivers down your spine
and imagined the soft dreams
that played in your head
The love I had for you was unfathomable
Lost in your spellbinding beauty

I crave a spontaneous
passionate and crazy love
that sets your soul on fire
and illuminates the whole world
-
Everybody will look in awe
and envy that love

-A love like this

12/1/15

I just sit and think about him
And i think to myself
"Wow, I fucking love him so much."
I love and am in love with everything
about him in this infinite moment
Every time I see his smile
I seem to fall in love all over again..

Did you forget how
my sweet love tastes
The kind of passion
that makes you ache
Did you forget the feeling
of my lips
My hips
My luminous love
which sparkles through
the hazy eclipse

-you never really *remembered*

"Are you still with that one guy?"
Someone asked me
A thousand memories
played through my head
I let out a soft smile and sighed
as I replied "No, I'm not."

-questions

When I met you

They say that when you know, you know
And I knew
Amidst the hazy amber glow
My soul was drawn to you

Don't be afraid of love
Share this happiness with me and
the simplicity of looking into
each other's eyes with
satisfaction in knowing
when we have nothing
we have each other

-Oh the irony

Spark

Looking at you sparks a
flame within my heart
Your soul ignites me
The smell of cologne in
the nape of your neck
makes me sparkle like champagne
Pull me in closer
Your *touch*
Your eyes
Your everything
Makes me burst like fireworks
How do you make me
feel so deeply?

Old wounds

You're the reason
I fear being close to people
The reason I push good people away
-
I give myself to the wrong people
in fear of pain
I ruin anything real at my grasp
in fear of it being torn away
In fear of watching it slowly slip away
Knowing there's nothing I can do
except watch it disintegrate
like your love did
-
Because of you
I know good things never stay

Your hands

Having been through so much
Held so much
Beaten and broken so beautifully
I'll never forget *your hands*
Pulling my waist
Grasping leg
Caressing my cheeks
Nobody will ever have your fingers
I adore your fingers
and the way you run them
through my hair
Delicately
Subtly

Storms

When all there seems to be
is sorrowful rain and
glum skies
Be your own light
Radiate this crestfallen town with
your spirit
Don't let the raindrops
put out the fire within your soul
Be the light
that guides the broken
and the damned
to *true* happiness

It is what it is

Sometimes we will have to be alone
Walk these stone pavements on our own
and that's okay
-
Haunted by old scars
New lovers
The hearts we were too afraid to risk
Opportunities left untaken
Words unspoken
Feelings un-expressed
-
Some people just don't come back
unless it is to haunt me
-
I am now content with loneliness
I enjoy my own company
It is what it is

Spectator

Watching from behind my walls
Hidden
Protected
Watching people *live*
I gaze through this two way mirror
But I am merely a spectator
unable to participate in
this event called life
-

I am confined
by the walls I've built
Patiently waiting for someone to
tear them down

Friendly reminder

You are
Worthy
Bold
Powerful
Capable of anything
you put your brilliant mind to
As long as you never stop
believing
-
Don't let anybody strip you
of your hope
You deserve so much more
You are so much more

Unashamed

Be prideful of the love you have to give
Not many can truly understand
the depths of it
Only a select few can carry it
Don't dilute your emotions
in order to be coequal with
someone else's Insubstantial love
Let your heart bloom
Share how deeply you feel
Be brave
courageous
and unashamed
in the way you love

Yours truly

-

This is my heart and soul at your fingertips
My passion
My wrath
My love
My hurting
My vulnerability and raw emotions
Illustrated through these poems
All *for you*

yours truly

Made in the USA
Middletown, DE
14 June 2017